Jump Starts

Jump Starts

30 SECOND LESSONS IN
LEADERSHIP FOR ALL OF US

Craig Olsen

RJCommunications
New York

ISBN 978-0-9799647-0-1

Published by C.J. Olsen

In cooperation with RJCommunications LLC, New York

Design and layout by SelfPublishing.com

Printed in the United States of America

Acknowledgement

I would like to acknowledge and thank everyone who encouraged and assisted me on this journey including Eric, Syd, Carmen, Karleen, Pat and Vaughan

I would like to especially thank my daughter Sarah for putting her technical writing skills to the ultimate test in editing this book.

Contents

Introduction

What is a Jump Start?

Jump Starts aren't newly conceived, revolutionary concepts. At some time or another you have likely heard most, if not all, of them. You will find yourself saying "Yeah, I knew that." The problem seems to be we have forgotten their significance while keeping pace in today's hectic world. When we don't practice the lessons we learned along the way, we tend to forget them. We all need a *Jump Start* to remind us of these key ideas in leadership and in life.

Vision

I have always marveled at a sculptor's ability to look at a piece of stone, envision objects encased within and then slowly, carefully chip away until the form emerges as a beautiful work of art. Most of us couldn't see what the stone could become, but the artist could. He had the vision to see what was not there and create, thru skill and effort, the finished product.

Leaders have that same visionary skill. They look at their company and see not only what is, but what can be. Leaders have the drive, the talent, the patience to create things others could only contemplate. Leaders invent, create, and build. They take the step forward and, like the sculptor, make the dream a reality.

If you want to be a leader, you must first possess the vision of what the end product will be. You have to be able to understand it, define it, and articulate it. Then, you have to implant that vision into others. They need to see what you see. If they don't know where you're going, it will be difficult to follow. The most successful companies are those where everyone understands and embraces the company's direction and goals.

Finally, you must use patience and skill to implement the vision you have. You must create the plans and objectives that will get you and your staff there. Those plans could include training, organization shifts, new products, new facilities or new personnel. It all equates to motivating the right people to get the job done and providing them with the tools and framework to do it.

Only then will your vision become a reality; a work of art.

A Smile in Your Voice

Few things are as irritating as trying to get information over the phone from someone who isn't smiling. How can you tell they aren't smiling? You can hear it in their voice. The "May I help you?" often sounds like a plea to just go away. I've managed call centers and my ear can spot a smile three rows away. A person who smiles on the phone projects the image of a friendly company – a company wanting to do business with you.

So ask yourself; when you answer the phone how do you sound? Are you gruff? Do you sound short? Does your voice make the caller regret he/she ever dialed your number?

Put on a smile. If necessary, put a mirror next the phone and glance into it before picking up the receiver or while you're talking. Is it the face of a friendly voice?

Craig Olsen

Attitudes about you and about your
company can be heard as well as seen. So
smile. Callers will hear it in your voice.

Believing You Can Win

Vince Lombardi, an icon in the NFL, once said "Winning is contagious…unfortunately so is losing". Every sports leader I've ever met will tell you that winning is as much a mental conquest as a physical one. Winning is the culmination of practice and training spurred on by the belief that you can, and will, succeed.

As a leader, what kind of energy and drive do you bring to the game? Are your positive actions and results spreading to the rest of your team or are you stuck in a downhill cycle? Are you just showing up or are you really digging in with the effort and confidence it takes to create a winning environment?

Take a moment to evaluate your strengths. Shore up those areas of your team that may be subject to weakness. For example, do you see complacency? Then create a sense of urgency in what your team is doing but not one of panic. Do you see skills that are missing? Then develop them through training and education. Once all the pieces are in place you need to eliminate the last obstacle – self doubt. It's a showstopper. Don't let it bring you or your team down.

Remember, in order to win, you must first believe you can.

Hitting Bottom

"I don't measure a man's success by how high he climbs but by how high he bounces when he hits bottom." ~ *General George S. Patton.*

Patton knew what he was talking about. After nearly destroying his military career over an incident which involved slapping an enlisted man, Patton went on to regain command and lead the U.S. 3rd Army across France and thru Germany during World War II. He bounced back and to this day remains one of the most successful field generals of any U.S. military campaign.

All of us face setbacks along the way – failing a test, not getting that promotion, losing a job. We all face low points. How you handle critical moments like these is what Patton was referring to. Do you wallow in the unfair nature of events or do you pick yourself up and move forward? Do you bemoan your fate or do you learn from it and regain your momentum with renewed purpose and understanding?

Setbacks occur. Sometimes they are of our own doing. Sometimes they are not. We can't win all the time. But leaders learn from those events and come back even stronger.

We have choices. We can lie on the ground when we fall or we can get up and climb even higher.

Everyday Courage

What is courage? Some define courage as heroism in the face of extreme dangers – the fire fighter rushing into a burning building to find a trapped child or rescuers braving a swollen river to save a stranded motorist. Courageous acts? Absolutely! But courage goes beyond those notable examples of selfless bravery. It exists beyond life or death scenarios.

Courage is the ability to conquer self doubt and then act with purpose and poise. Courage can be stepping up to a podium to make that first speech, going back to school to finish a degree or simply applying for a new job.

We all have self doubts. We all have fears – be they real or imagined. And we can all be courageous. Courage, everyday courage, is the conviction of spirit and will despite overwhelming doubt. Courage isn't a lack of fear. It is the mastery over it.

How do you measure up? Do you shirk in the face of these fears or do you summon the courage & conviction to act? How can you give yourself that "edge" to master those inner demons? Start by:

> ➤ Preparing – Gather as much knowledge as you can. Practice. Anticipate.

> ➤ Focusing on the result – Look beyond the immediate swirl around you.

> ➤ Acting – Swallow lingering doubt and move forward. Nothing happens without you.

Be courageous and make it happen.

Asking for Help

A wily old salesman I knew always
complained about how tough the market
was or how difficult his new quotas were.
Yet he always seemed to make his sales
numbers and then some. During a
conversation, I asked him what his secret
was. He replied he merely asked for help.
"Get someone to do a favor for you and
they're your friend for life," he would say.
Pretty simple, pretty profound.

Asking for help is never an easy thing to do.
In this world of self reliance, people tend to
think asking for help somehow shows
weakness. Nothing could be further from
the truth. By asking someone for advice we
show respect for their opinions and
abilities. We elevate the individual and
build a foundation for partnership. More
often than not, the simple act of asking for
help will yield far more positive results

than imagined and a willingness to help you again in the future. Once someone has helped you by virtue of advice or action they have, in a sense, accepted a vested interest in your success. You are now elevated in their eyes as well. They want you to succeed.

So put aside the concern that you look less than perfect and ask for help. The answer you get will yield benefits for a long, long while.

Hearing What Was Said

Do you remember the children's game "telephone"? One child would think of a word or phrase and whisper it into the next child's ear. That child would then pass it along to the next in line and so on. It was always humorous to see what the last child heard compared to what the first one had said.

As a game when we were children, it was fun. In the grown-up world, it isn't. Far too often we come across situations where people just assume what they said (or thought they said) was perceived by the listener in exactly the same way the speaker envisioned. That doesn't always happen. In fact, having our words interpreted exactly as we intended probably occurs less often than we realize. It's not just the words we use. Our tone, pace, facial expressions and even body language play important roles in how we are interpreted as well.

How can you reduce potential confusion? Here are some tips:

- ➤ Paraphrase. If you are unsure everyone understands, repeat your message using different wording.

- ➤ Ask questions. Whether listening or speaking, it's a way to clarify.

- ➤ Don't assume everyone knows all the details about the subject. (See above)

- ➤ Above all, show patience. Not everyone absorbs information at the same speed.

Remember, what you say doesn't always matter. It's what everyone thought you said that does.

Good, Better, Best

Some of the most important (and most useful) life lessons we learn come from simple things we were taught in grade school. Not just how to sit quietly and pay attention in class or how to get along with the kid next to you. Those are important too. I'm talking about the phrases or stories we remember because your teacher thought them important. Life lessons cleverly disguised in rhymes and verse. We didn't know exactly what they meant, but we memorized them anyway. Not only did they teach us to get along with everyone else, but they taught us to get along with ourselves. This was Ms. Erdmann's favorite.

> Good, better, best
> Never let it rest
> Until the good is better
> And the better is best.

It goes beyond improving your penmanship or learning your math tables. It says don't accept just being okay. Be better – whether it's taking a grade school spelling test or developing spaceships for NASA. All of us have abilities and all of us should take each one and strive to make them better.

Then go make them the best.

Perception is Reality

A recent series of ads for a large camera company hammered home the phrase "image is everything". While the company was trying to reinforce the power of pictures and their product, the true importance of image goes further than just another commercial. Corporations (and individuals) are constantly trying to enhance their image. Why? Because people want to know that the goods and services they select have value. They want to know they are getting what they paid for. The companies behind those goods and services know the public will seek the person or product they trust – the ones with the right image.

What can you do to improve your or your company's image? What can you do to better the company's products or services? It can start by simply saying "Good morning" on the phone to a caller instead of "Hello".

If someone does express concern about you, your company or its products pay attention. Image is something to be fiercely guarded. Work at it. Don't dismiss criticisms of any kind as unjustified. Maybe they are. Maybe they're not. But they are criticisms nonetheless and will alter the perception of you or your company. It's the perception that really matters.

We need all the advantages we can muster just to compete in today's world. Don't let even the slightest criticism go unheeded. Fix the criticism or fix the perception. Image is everything. Perception is reality.

The Scarcest Resource

Ask any leader what is the one thing they wish they had more of and the answer is likely to be time. The father of modern management, Peter Drucker, said, "Time is the scarcest resource and unless it is managed, nothing else can be managed."

How well do you manage that scarce and precious resource? Do you find at the end of the day there just wasn't enough time to get through everything? Are you constantly caught juggling too many tasks? Are you in an ongoing tradeoff between professional and personal responsibilities? Here are a few suggestions.

> ➤ Before you leave the office at the end of the day, make a list of those things you want to get done tomorrow. Put them in order by priority. Move uncompleted tasks

from today to the top of tomorrow's list.

➤ When you hit the office door in the morning, start at the top of the list and focus on that task's completion. Get it done. Then go to the next one.

➤ Don't review an item and then set it aside to complete later. Handle it now. Otherwise you will have wasted that initial review time by having to re-review later.

➤ When you have finished a task, check it off the list. You'll be surprised how good it feels.

Manage your time or become a slave to its short supply.

Communicate, Communicate, Communicate

If the old adage for success in real estate is "location, location, location", in management it's "communication, communication, communication". The one consistent stumbling block to success I witness in companies large and small, is the inconsistent, or more often non existent, communication of the company's goals and objectives to its workforce - the very people that are driving the production end of the business.

In order to do a good job, everyone needs to know not only what is expected of them, but how their job fits into the overall framework of the company. Clarity to staff is critical. However, the communication shouldn't end there. Upward communication is just as important. The view from all levels of personnel can provide valuable insights to gaining improved efficiencies, more accurate results, better customer satisfaction and a stronger bottom line. Effective dialog is not always easy and certainly not always expedient. But without ongoing communication – upstream and down – you have limited the likelihood of your company's success and your own. Take the time to make certain everyone knows not just what to do and how to do it, but why it is important.

Communicate, communicate, communicate! We'll all learn something.

Promises Made, Promises Kept

Very few things in business (or in life) can be as frustrating as waiting for something that had been promised to be completed by a certain time, yet wasn't. I'm not just talking about furniture delivery or a dentist appointment, but a much broader arena. It can be a promise to return a call or a commitment to get a report compiled. When we're late, it says several things - none of which are very good.

First of all, being late implies that we haven't managed our time very well. Perhaps we took on too much or perhaps simply underestimated the task. In either case, we weren't able to finish the job when expected. Maybe it was just Murphy's law, maybe it wasn't.

Second, when we're late, we put an undo burden on those who were depending on us.

If someone needed your results to do their job, by not getting the data to them on time you are likely causing them to have problems.

Finally, when you're late you have said your schedule is more important than the person (or people) who are waiting on you.

We all know delays happen. When you're going to be late, let the people who are waiting for you (or your project) know well enough in advance so they can adjust their schedules too. Don't simply assume they will 'understand'.   Demonstrate you have concern for their time and their commitments as well as your own whether it's a client, your boss, your staff or your family.

The Size of the Prize

A contest was held during a regional meeting of salesmen for a large company. The prize was relatively insignificant - a mere ten dollars. However, when the sales manager announced the results, the winner wasn't just handed a ten dollar bill in an envelope. Instead, he was asked to come up to the front of the group and hold out his hands. The manager then proceeded to slowly drop ten silver dollars into his cupped hands one at a time. With every clink the entire audience became more mesmerized. By the time the last coin landed everyone in the room was cheering. They all wanted to be the one getting that prize. They all wanted to win. It was only ten dollars, but it had a ten thousand dollar impact.

It's not just the size of the prize that counts, it's also the manner in which it's presented.

All it takes is a reinforcing emphasis on the impact of the presentation, not just the reward. It doesn't have to be a pile of silver dollars to make an impression. If you are giving someone a certificate of achievement, frame it first. Better yet, make it into a plaque. Make the event a "big deal". Make the presentation in front of everyone. The return you get for that extra investment will resonate for years.

If It Ain't Broke

The old adage goes, "If it ain't broken, don't fix it." While this piece of advice may hold true for household plumbing, applying the same principle to our job or company is a sure fire recipe for disaster. Even when we're on the right track, if we stand still long enough we'll get hit by a freight train. Time (and competition) stands still for no one.

Change is not only good for a company, it's an absolute necessity. The same can be said for you as well. Leaders need to constantly evaluate where they are, what they're doing and where they want to go. We should always be ready and willing to adapt to changes the job may require. Most people resist change. They find it is easier to stay with what they're doing in that "comfort zone". Don't let that happen to you. Changes are coming and just ignoring them is inviting failure.

Companies can be the same way. Complacency over success is a blight. Just because your firm succeeded once, don't think the effort level that got you there is no longer necessary. Every company out there wants to have the success you now enjoy. Everyone is looking for newer, faster, more efficient ways to do the same job you're doing today. They're creating new and better products to replace yours. Don't let that happen.

Create, redesign, renew, reinvent. Even if it isn't broken, fix it anyway.

Eating an Elephant

Sometimes the mountain of paperwork in front of you appears to be insurmountable. Perhaps the new sales quotas look unreachable. In times like these we all need to remember the answer to the old question, "How do you eat an elephant?" You eat an elephant one bite at a time.

The most difficult part of any large endeavor is sometimes just figuring out where to start. In the face of huge tasks or projects, here are a few tips to bring them down to size.

> ➤ Get a clear understanding of what the final result should be and when it needs to be completed. If you have questions about either, ask.

> ➤ Break that mountain of paperwork into several sections then set goals

for each one. Let others know what the steps are and keep them posted on your progress.

➤ Celebrate the completion of each step. Reward those who helped (you may need their help later on.)

➤ Take time to review along the way. Get feedback. Are you on time? Have any overall priorities shifted?

Conquer that elephant – one bite at a time.

Making it Right

We all have times when things don't go
exactly as planned. It happens. Whether
people are ill, the computer goes down or
there was an accident on your commuting
route. As a result of these unexpected
setbacks, you (or your company) will fail to
deliver and the complaints will roll in.
Whether the disgruntled folks are your
company's customers or in department
down the hall, they're not getting the
product or service they expected. The
phone will be ringing and you know some
angry voice will be on the other end. What
do you say? What do you do?

Never make the assumption your caller will
be soothed by hearing about your problems.
Absolutely no one wants excuses. The fact
you're even having the conversation is
already an indication of the caller's
frustration. Giving excuses only serves to

fan the flames of smoldering tensions. How do you gain control?

First apologize for any problems (regardless of who was at fault) and then ask what you can do to make it right. You won't be able to placate everyone, but you'll solve the complaint far more often than not.

People don't want to hear why their need wasn't met. They simply want to know how you're going to fix their problem. Just ask "what can I do to make it right," and you will.

You Don't Understand

In meetings and in general discussions few words get a person's dander up faster than the phrase, "You don't understand." Why? Because every time you say it you imply the other individual can't or won't see your reasoning. Perhaps they <u>do</u> understand or perhaps they don't. It really doesn't matter. You have drawn that line in the sand and said, "I'm right, you must be wrong." You have implied the fault in the discussion was not yours, but theirs for not "understanding" what you said. You have assumed the other person should have heard and processed everything you said exactly the way you *thought* you said it.

How do you avoid that negative reaction? Take responsibility. Remember, you are trying to convince someone else of your viewpoint. Any real problem is likely due to your explanation and not to their "understanding". Don't shift blame to someone else – whether it was your fault or not. Instead of saying "You don't understand," say "I didn't make that clear" or "I didn't say that right" and then rephrase your thoughts. When you put responsibility back where it truly belongs (on yourself), people are more willing to listen and accept your ideas.

Showing Up

Everyone knows the story surrounding the 2000 presidential election. George W. Bush beat Al Gore in Florida by a mere 537 votes giving Mr. Bush the state and the election. We know about the disputed vote counts and hanging chads. What seemed to be lost in the melee that followed (and is still being debated today) was only 50.6%[i] of the eligible voters in the state of Florida bothered to go to the polls. Only 68.1% of Florida's eligible voters had ever bothered to register! Nationally it wasn't much better. Only 51.3% of eligible voters in this country managed to vote across all fifty states. Mr. Bush won 47.9% of those votes cast for president that year. That means the election was decided by less than 25% of the eligible voters in the United States. Neither political party really won. Apathy did.

---

[i] P. 35 from David Leip's *Atlas of U.S. Presidential Elections*

If you want to make a difference, you have to show up. All of the preparation, all of the talk, all of the hype are useless unless you show up.

It's not just elections where apathy wins. It's the things you do everyday. If you didn't bother to attend a meeting because you thought it unimportant, you have no one to blame but yourself for a resulting outcome that doesn't suit you. You can't make much of an impact when you aren't there. No one is swayed by an argument that isn't made, a position that isn't represented or a vote that isn't cast. If you didn't care enough to be there, how can you expect anyone to care what you think, say or do now?

Start a trend. Show up. It may just change the course of history.

Setting a Good Example

The things we do define us. Our beliefs, our thoughts, our words all take a back seat to our actions. We can pretend to lead by telling others what they should or shouldn't do, but truly being a leader is setting the proper example for others to follow. What kind of leader are you? What kind of example do you provide to those around you at work? At home? Do you do the right thing all the time or only when someone is looking? Do you fudge expense reports or do you only turn in valid expenses? Are you really researching a report or just web surfing? Did you really give the project 100% of your attention and energy or were you just 'mailing in' your effort? Did you show up for your son's soccer game or was that round of golf more important?

If you want to make an impact and want to be the person that inspires others, you have to send the right message. You have to do the right thing and not just the expedient one. You have to be a good example.

If you can't (or won't), you'll be nothing more than a terrible warning.

Lights, Camera, Action

At the beginning of the Civil War the Union
military was barely functional. Most of the
troops available were in the western
reaches of the country. Abraham Lincoln
appointed General George McClellen to
create and command the forces that would
become known as the Army of the Potomac.
The general was a brilliant planner and
organizer. He built a magnificent
organization of 900,000 men backed by the
best engineering and industrial support the
then modern world had seen. McClellen's
army was not only better equipped, it was
twice the size of his Confederate opponents.
However, barely eighteen months after he
took charge, he lost his job. Why?

Despite all of his brilliance, McClellen
lacked the conviction to move forward into
battle. His inability to be decisive and

aggressive under pressure not only cost him his job, but nearly cost the Union the war.

How do you face a challenge? Do you meet it head on or do you hold back? Have you developed the perfect product or created the most efficient organization yet can't seem to get ahead? Preparation is only that – preparation. Your work is all for naught unless you use it to act. No one will know or appreciate your efforts if you don't put them into play. Move ahead. Act! You can't win the war if you don't engage the opposition. McClellen proved it.

Be There

Few things are more frustrating than
having to wait on someone to show up for
an appointment, a meeting, or an interview.
All of us can get caught in traffic, have car
problems, forget to set an alarm or just
plain forget. However, there's always a
telephone to let those waiting on you know
you are going to be late. Repeatedly not
showing up on time is an almost certain
way to alienate everyone. Excuses only go
so far and assuming "everyone knows that's
just the way I am" won't cut it either. Not
being there when you're expected tells
anyone who was waiting that they just
weren't important enough for you to plan
ahead. Consistently showing up late for
work tells your firm that you don't care
about your job. It's rude, disrespectful and
a sure fire way to hasten your departure
from the company. Your job performance
may be first class, but it does little to erase

the adverse impression you're leaving by
not being there when you should be.

Don't think showing up on time for work is
the only place that counts. The same can
be said for PTA meetings, church services
or your son's little league game. Plan well
enough in advance to allow for problems in
transportation, weather, etc. Be conscious
of the adverse impact you're having and
then work to keep your commitments.

Just be there and be on time.

Teaching Them to Fish

There is an old religious proverb that goes "Give a man a fish and you have fed him for a day. Teach a man to fish and you have fed him for a lifetime." The lesson is just as meaningful today when dealing with people, particularly subordinates. Sure, doing a task yourself may be more expedient than taking the time to explain it to someone else. Correcting an error someone made on a report may be easier than sitting down with the author and showing him/her where the mistakes are and how to avoid them. However, by doing it yourself you have lost an opportunity to teach how the task should be done. Even worse, you have reinforced the message that something less than complete is acceptable.

Take the time to pass your knowledge to others. Showing others how to do the job correctly may not be the easiest or most convenient thing to do, but the long term returns will be enormous. Be certain to question them along the way. Don't gloss over the explanation to ensure they understand the 'why' and not just the 'how'.

Don't just feed them the answer, teach them to fish.

Explaining Things

The noted actor Denzel Washington played attorney Joe Miller in the movie *Philadelphia.* When confronted with a complex or confusing situation Miller would interrupt and say, "Explain that to me like I was an eight year old." Miller wasn't trying to be demeaning nor was he slow to understand. He just wanted a clear explanation in simplistic terms and language.

Do you fall into the same category as the people Joe Miller was talking to? When you try to explain a position or make a presentation are you met with blank stares or befuddled expressions? We are all guilty of overstating at times. We are so certain everyone knows exactly what we are talking about, we get lost in the complexities of our own explanation. We try to impress. We provide too much detail.

When trying to get a message across to people, the last thing we want to do is lose them in a wave of acronyms, graphs or complex analyses. Here are some suggestions to avoid the glazed eye look from your audience.

> ➢ Keep it short. There is no need for a long explanation where none is required.

> ➢ Keep it simple. Avoid long or confusing language. Avoid buzzwords or acronyms.

> ➢ Keep it on point. Don't drift into other topics or provide non essential data.

> ➢ Keep repeating. Summarize. If at all unsure, paraphrase.

The best explanation is one everyone understands.

Fact or Opinion

Today's world is full of conjecture , innuendo and outright misleading information. Sit through a half dozen political commercials during an election year and you will understand. Defining where the truth ends and speculation begins isn't always easy. The line is so often blurred it is difficult to tell what is fact and what isn't.

Do you embellish your numbers or use statistics that simply aren't there to 'sell' your ideas or products? Do you blur the lines between fact and fiction? Stop! Before you toss in that reference to something you *think* is correct, check it out. Is it fact or just opinion?

Facts are things we know to be true. The earth is round, 2+2=4, etc. Facts are backed up by hard, cold evidence. Opinions, on the other hand, are things we *believe* are valid, but cannot prove. "The facts, ma'am. Just the facts," may be an old *Dragnet* cliché, but should be taken as gospel when creating reports or making presentations. Your work should be fact based. Opinions are acceptable *only* where stated as such. When opinions are used as facts they become the fodder of lawsuits for fraud or misrepresentation. If you are unsure something is truly a fact either state it as your opinion or don't use it at all.

Everyone is entitled to their own opinions. No one is entitled to their own facts.

Any Road Will Take You There

I once worked for a CEO who was extremely fond of using literary quotations and applying them to business principles. One of his favorites (and mine) came from Lewis Carroll's *'Alice Through the Looking Glass'*. When a very lost Alice asks the White Rabbit which way she should go, he replies, "When you don't know where you want to go, any road will take you there."

"Where do you want to go?" sounds so simple, so basic. Yet individuals (and companies as well) often get caught up in crises of the day or focus only on immediate results. They get pulled away by so many distractions, they quickly lose sight of the long term goals they set for themselves (and their firms).

How do we get back on track? Start by determining what your destination is.

Maybe the goal is to retire at fifty five or perhaps it's running your own firm. Whatever the destination is, define it. Verbalize what you want to accomplish. Write it down. Memorize it. Refer back to it often. If the vision is a company one, be certain that your employees know it and understand its importance.

The daily roads we choose and decisions we make become far clearer and much easier when we understand where we really want to go.

The School Bus Syndrome

There was always at least one kid who seemed to wait to start his homework until he was on the bus heading towards school. He always had an excuse for not beginning earlier, but somehow you knew he just didn't have a sense of urgency or he was easily distracted. His homework looked exactly the way you expected – sloppy, incomplete and generally wrong.

Do you have that school bus syndrome? You can't seem to focus on things that need to be done until the very last minute? Then, when you finally get to the task, is the result fragmented and incomplete?

Don't think others won't notice a "school bus syndrome" job. They will. Maybe your daring and nonchalance impressed the curly haired girl next to you in grade school, but it won't empress your employers. Every time you stall on a task until the last possible moment, you're saying either the job wasn't important enough to plan for or, worse, you don't have the ability to prioritize the things you do. Neither message is a good one.

Don't wait for the school bus to start working on those tasks. Make a priority list. Put events/tasks on a calendar and check tomorrow's needs today. Better yet, check out those things due next week.

It's a grown up world. Excuses like "the dog ate my homework" don't work anymore.

Change It

I run into people everyday who rant about
how bad their life is. They hate their job,
they don't get proper respect at work, they
don't like the school their children are in,
etc. Nothing seems to make them happy.
Unfortunately, they would rather complain
about their life than change it. Perhaps all
they want is sympathy or perhaps they
really do want to change.

Life doesn't have an 'easy' button. Change
takes effort and resolve. Changing careers
may require going back to school or getting
more training. You may have to start over
in a new company or in a new location. No
'easy' button there. If you are truly
unhappy in what you are doing, you will
never be successful. Turn it around.
Change. Find something you are
passionate about doing and go for it. No
one wants to hear constant complaining,

but friends and family will jump to your support if you make a sincere effort to change your current status.

Life is far too short to spend time doing something you hate.

Do as I Pay, Not as I Say

A consultant I know was helping a company restructure the commission policy of their sales force. While volume figures were good, unit prices were down and expenses were dramatically out of line. All this was in spite of numerous edicts handed down from headquarters to push higher margined product lines and cut back on spending. Things weren't turning out as the corporate leaders envisioned. Just how do you get employees to do what you want?

The consultant put it bluntly. "Do as I pay, not as I say." Create programs to encourage others to act the way you want them to act. Whether it's a commissioned salesman, an order entry clerk or your warehouse manager, everyone will act in their own long term best interests. If those interests are in line with the company's objectives, all is well and good. However, when the best interests of the individual are in conflict with those of the company, look out. Don't expect the individual to act in ways contrary to their personal interests. It just won't happen. Commission plans, incentive programs and performance or salary reviews should always tie the pay of the employee directly to the needs of the company.

Do as I pay, not as I say.

The Ox Has Been Gored

In the midst of a *very* long business meeting one attendee brought up topic that been discussed at great length and where a decision had already been reached. He insisted on revisiting his stance on the subject yet again. Everyone was tired of hearing the same arguments over and over. The mood was tense. The leader of the group looked at him and simply said, "The ox has been gored and the cart's in the ditch, move on." Everyone roared with laughter and the tension vanished. While the phrase got everyone's attention and a good laugh, it's part of a valuable lesson.

When the settlers of the old West were traveling across America and almost any kind of calamity befell them (including losing an ox and a wagon), they continued to press forward. The settlers couldn't afford the luxury to argue about something which already occurred or a decision already made. The settlers had to move on or risk not completing the journey at all.

If we allow ourselves to get caught up in constant rehashing every event that went wrong, every decision made or action taken, we will never reach our goals. Bring up important questions, discuss them and weigh alternatives. Everyone needs to hear and understand the issues and learn from past mistakes. However, once a decision is made, move on. Going forward is in everyone's best interest. There are far too many mountains to climb to be dwelling on things that will not change.

Perspective

While watching one of those home
remodeling shows, I was struck by how one
person's perception of tasteful decorating
was trashed as gaudy and completely out of
touch by someone else. Neither individual
could be considered wholly accurate. It was
a matter of perception by each of them.
Their opinions were based upon what each
saw. The author Anais Nin put it a little
more succinctly, "We don't see things as
they are. We see things as we are."

Her words are valuable advice when
dealing with others. Just because
someone's viewpoint or opinion differs from
yours doesn't automatically make them
wrong. They may just have a different
perspective on the subject. Their
background, education and experiences are
never going to exactly match yours. Why
should their viewpoints? Your beliefs and

opinions are just that – your beliefs and opinions. They aren't necessarily facts. As long as there is room for interpretation, other people's views merit consideration. You don't have to agree with them, just take them into account.

Of course, that's just my perspective.

Making Mistakes

Ok, you made a mistake. Everybody makes mistakes. Maybe the error was little one with little consequence or maybe it was very large one with equally large consequences. Regardless, the mistake happened and it was your fault. The question is, now what are you going to do? You could ignore it, but that won't change the fact that it happened. You could try to shift the blame to someone or something else and claim it was beyond your control, but you know that really wasn't the case either. Simply said, you need to learn from what occurred and then move on.

Blaming someone else or just ignoring the error ever happened won't help you avoid making the same mistake all over again. Accept the responsibility that you did something wrong and then examine the circumstances surrounding it. For

example, if you get a bad review at work,
listen to why you were rated poorly and ask
what you can do about it. Just denying the
problem was your fault won't solve
anything. Understand how to avoid
making the same missteps in the future.

Mistakes are lessons wrapped in veils of
regret. Learn from them but don't let them
cloud your vision or your future. Take
action and make the changes necessary to
avoid repeating a problem and then move
on. Just stewing about events that have
already occurred is simply a waste of time
and energy.

The past cannot change but tomorrow can
be whatever you want to make it.

Thank You

Sometimes the simplest things can have the most impact. Yet, how often do we forget to do them? Giving recognition for a job well done, a favor granted or a compliment made can be as easy as saying "Thank you." A smile and meaningful "Thank you" doesn't just brighten someone's day, it acknowledges their effort was not taken for granted. Whether it's a co-worker, the waitress at lunch or someone in your family, all of us need to be reminded that what we do is appreciated; that it's important. Using just a simple thank you in a note, a card, an email or a simple verbal "thanks," can reinforce good behavior and a positive attitude.

Show your gratitude. Make certain to hand out "Thank you's" liberally. Spread them around at work, home and in the community. Demonstrate you acknowledge and appreciate the efforts others have made.   Not only will brighten their day, it will wind up brightening yours as well.

Filling the Quiet Void

The ability to sit quietly with your thoughts and wait for the other person to say something is often referred to as the mastery of silence. You could be in a contract negotiation, a job interview or a meeting of your peers. In these instances when there is a prolonged period of silence anxiety builds. You may feel the need to fill that quiet void with some pertinent or witty remark.

Be careful. While some of these periods of silence are unplanned, others are intentional. They can be an attempt to get you to lower your guard. When you say something, anything, if not required may be perceived as a weakness or an annoyance – particularly in negotiations or a sales pitch. Sometimes silence is indeed golden. So keep those thoughts under wraps. Don't let everyone know what you are thinking all of the time. Unless the situation calls for an answer, suggestion or comment, keep your thoughts to yourself.

When you fill uncomfortable silence by blurting out some unneeded comment, your action just may have said a lot more than your words.

The Lost Art of Writing a Letter

My brother is a business professor at a small mid western college. We both lament long and often how even the brightest students coming through the college ranks today fail in one of the fundamental abilities demanded by business - writing a letter.

In the era of texting and email, few individuals seem to be learning this basic skill. Indeed, a lot has changed in the business world over the last thirty years. However, the ability to write sound, well crafted letters is still a most valued and fundamental tool. Well structured business letters are keys to getting a job, developing proposals and thanking customers for their loyalty. Letters are the embodiment of you, the writer, in the reader's eyes. A letter represents your ability to structure your thoughts, coherently express those thoughts and to do so with grace and style.

Do you write clear missives or are they jumbled and disjointed ramblings? Here are some suggestions:

> When composing the body of a letter, first state 1) what you want, 2) why you want it and 3) what you want again.

> Read your letter aloud. Does it 'sound' like you? You'll be surprised how many times simple syntax errors will jump off the page when spoken.

> When reading your letter aloud, if you have to take a breath in mid sentence, the sentence is too long. Consider making two shorter ones.

> Check your spelling. Pay particular attention to those things 'spell check' doesn't know. For example, proper

names or the difference between words like 'weight' and 'wait'.

If the writing isn't clear, what does it say about the person who wrote it?

Being S.M.A.R.T.

There are many, many articles books on how to manage people. How do we set effective goals and give direction to the individuals who support us? One of the best methods I have come across is to just be "smart". In this case, it's the acronym S.M.A.R.T. and it stands for Specific, Measurable, Attainable, Related and Time bound.

Specific - The task should be clear and the expected results exacting. People need to know what is considered acceptable and what is not.

Measurable - If we can't calculate the results, what have we accomplished? Results can be productivity measures, increased sales or reduced customer complaints. However, they have to be measurable.

Attainable - It does no good to set a goal that can't be reached. It discourages your employees. The result must be within their capabilities even if that goal is a stretch.

Related - Make certain the goals or tasks are in line with the person's job. Don't expect sales personnel to become accountants or vice versa.

Time Bound - Tasks having no targeted ending generally won't be completed when you expect them to be (if ever). Your staff needs to know when the task is supposed to be finished.

If everyone on the team has a S.M.A.R.T. understanding of the task or project, not only will the likelihood of success sharply increase, but personnel evaluations become less strenuous for you and certainly more productive. After all, everything was clearly defined in advance.

Finally, being S.M.A.R.T. goes beyond your staff. Apply S.M.A.R.T. to personal and corporate goals as well. It helps everyone focus better. After all, it's the smart thing to do.

Hiring Winners

I am not the biggest Donald Trump fan in the world, but I have to admire the man's decision making ability. He can see thru the clutter and make tough, straight forward decisions - particularly when it comes to the people he has surrounding him. He puts his philosophy this way, "I don't want losers working for me and you shouldn't want losers working for you." I agree.

Far too often, in all levels of management, people intentionally surround themselves with individuals of a lesser caliber. People think by doing so, no one will be usurping their knowledge or leadership. They think they won't be threatened and their job will be secure. This just isn't the case

The most successful leaders will tell you to surround yourself with an aggressive, bright staff. Not only will they keep you 'on your toes', they'll make you look good along they way. After all, you hired them!

Don't tolerate losers. Hire and maintain winners. You and your company will be the better for it.

Praise in Public

Have you ever been witness to someone being "dressed down" by a co-worker or supervisor? Even though it wasn't directed at you, chances are you wanted crawl into the nearest corner and disappear. Perhaps a reprimand was warranted, but humiliation never is.

Reprimands should be done without an audience. If the report was late, the figures were incorrect or the wrong equipment got delivered, the individual needs to know that their actions were unacceptable. However, they don't need to be embarrassed in front of others. When you are reprimanding someone, do it away from others or behind closed doors. A public reprimand hurts the moral of everyone when it happens, not just the person who made the mistake.

On the flip side, when giving praise to someone for a job well done, do it in a crowd. Make it a big deal. The self esteem of that person will not only go up, it will soar. Open praise will also give everyone else who is a witness to it a boost of their own and a renewed effort to get into the limelight themselves.

Praise in public. Punish in private.

Too Many Balls in the Air

Circus jugglers are impressive. They are seemingly able to defy gravity by keeping six or seven balls in the air at the same time. Not many of us can match that skill, but a lot of us seem to try. We take on too many tasks and try to be all things to all people. Unlike the circus juggler, very few people (or companies) can effectively "juggle" more than two or three projects at the same time. If we try, the result is likely to be dropping not just one "ball", but all of them. How can you cope with multiple tasks?

Set up your priorities, personal or corporate, and focus on only the top two items. Put all of your energies into doing those two things well and don't be sidetracked by other events around you. If those other events were really important, they would have been at the top of the list to begin with. You simply can't be everything to everyone. Stay the course. Let everyone around you, especially your staff, know what the priorities are. Focus on them. Don't allow others to throw more balls into the air until you have taken care of those already in flight.

Polish Your Shoes

It is often said clothes do not make the man (or woman) and how people dress should not be held against them. These sayings may be true in other areas but in the business world neatness counts. Your appearance is the first impression others will have. Starting from that first image, people will form opinions and make decisions about you. Right or wrong as those opinions may be, it happens.

What kind of an impression do you make? Are you conveying the message of a professional or does your food stained, three day old shirt tell a different tale? You don't have to own a designer wardrobe or a different suit for every day of the month. You can and should, however, take a few steps to put your best foot forward. We probably (and hopefully) all remember to wash our hands and face and brush our teeth. These are "no brainers". However, what about polished shoes and a pressed shirt (not just a clean one)? Is your hair combed? Is your tie free from the lunch you had earlier? Are your slacks pressed or did the crease vanish months ago?

If you expect to lead others, dress accordingly. The care you show in yourself and your appearance reflects on everything you do. The image you create is all part of the package.

Appearances count. Now go polish those shoes.

Going Out on a Limb

We would all like to be in a profession where success comes easily and without risk or effort. Unfortunately, most of us have yet to find such an idyllic calling. After all, there is a reason they call it work. That's not to say we shouldn't enjoy what we do for a living, just don't lose sight of the fact that effort and risk are going to be part of it.

To be successful we have to do things we haven't done before. We have to learn new ideas and concepts. We can't close our minds to change or avoid every risk that comes along. The American humorist Will Rogers said, "You've got to go out on a limb sometimes because that's where the fruit is." We all look for the low hanging, easy to grab results. However very often the sweetest ones are not within our immediate grasp. The only way to get those elusive rewards is to climb the tree and go out on that limb. Take chances. Reach beyond what you're doing today to make a better tomorrow. Stretch. Grow.

The taste of success is really only as sweet as the reach and effort made to get it.

Everyone Sells

All of us are in sales. We may not be selling widgets to ACME manufacturing, but we are all selling. The product can be something tangible or an idea you are presenting in a meeting. Your pitch can be for a design for something new or a concept from an era gone by. The point is, we are always out there convincing others our ideas and opinions are worthy of their consideration. These actions make us all salespeople – whether we aspire to be or not. So for all of you sales guys, here are some basic "rules of the road:"

> ➢ Know your product – whether it's tangible or ideal. Remember, if you're in an interview, you are the product.

> ➢ You won't always make a sale, but the better prepared you are, the greater the likelihood of winning.

> ➢ When you have actually made the sale – stop selling. Countless sales have been lost because of not knowing when to stop.

Now, go sell something.

Fixing the Problem

Everywhere you turn, people are quick to point out faults in others. The topic of criticism could be government spending, a new corporate policy or the latest PTA project. Pointing out problems in others or bemoaning lack of effective control doesn't require a lot of effort. It's the old "everyone talks about the weather but no one does anything about it". To paraphrase that observation, "everyone likes to complain about problems around them, but very few do anything to fix them".

How do you approach the corporate or community environment you live in? Are you quick to point out problems but slow to provide answers? Do you take "pot shots" from the sidelines, but never aim at the remedies to actually fix the issues faced by those around you?

Anyone can complain. We need people with intelligence and understanding to dig in and ferret out problems and issues. To be a leader, to truly make a difference, successful people will not just identify issues, they will solve them.

Leaders don't just point out the problems. They work out the solutions as well.

Waiting for the Perfect Pitch

It was Lee Iacocca, the former head of Chrysler, who said "I have always found that if I move with seventy-five percent or more of the facts that I usually never regret it. It's the guys who want to have everything perfect that drive you crazy". Are you one of the guys who would drive Iacocca crazy? Do you hesitate turning in a proposal or handing in a budget because it isn't "perfect"? Are you caught holding back while trying to convince yourself more needs to be rechecked or reanalyzed or reworded? Or are you able to "get off the dime" and get things moving?

In baseball if you waiting for the perfect pitch, you're likely to be called out on strikes before you ever swing the bat. They call it a strike "zone", not a strike "spot". That zone is what Iacocca was talking

about. The information may not be perfect
or complete, but you have to swing at it.

Successful people don't wait for the perfect
pitch. They start swinging when they are
comfortable the ball will be in the "zone".
They take the calculated chance. They act.
They go for it.

Don't always wait for the perfect pitch.
That ball might just sail by you for strike
three.

Count to Ten

We're human beings and emotions, including anger, are part of the package. Anger can be a great motivator. Yet more often anger leads us to do or say things we ultimately regret. This is especially true in the office environment. Whole careers can be ruined in seconds by the angry response to some perceived wrong – whether the wrong was real or not.

What do you do when someone angers you at work? How can you avoid doing something ill advised in the tension of the moment? Here are some suggestions;

> ➢ Count to ten (or twenty) before saying or doing anything. If the situation requires a response, write it down first, go get a cup of coffee, come back and re-read it. Only then respond and only if necessary.

➢ If possible, take the notes you had written (see above) and put them in your desk until tomorrow.

➢ Channel your anger into understanding what happened. Circumstances are not always what they initially appear to be. Did the offender have all of the current information? Anger is a waste of energy unless channeled.

➢ Evaluate *all* the impacts of your response. Not just on yourself, but on others in your company and your family.

Don't let the heat of the moment burn you for a lifetime.

The First Thirty Seconds

It has been estimated during a job interview or a sales pitch you have only ten minutes to make an impression. Some have said you have only five minutes. The truth is you have about 30 seconds. The rest of the time the person sitting behind the desk is seeking to validate his/her initial decision. Is it fair? Probably not, but it happens. What can you do to throw the odds in your favor? Here are some tips:

> ➤ Never, ever be late. The 30 seconds will be clicking away if you're there or not. Camp out on the doorstep for an hour if you have to, but don't be late!

> ➤ Never show up more than 10 minutes early. It's extremely rude as well. (See above about camping on the doorstep)

➢ Always "overdress". It doesn't matter that everyone else is in polo shirts. If this is your first time there, you should be in a dress shirt and tie.

➢ Always check the mirror before you walk in. The salad you had for lunch should never be a part of your smile.

➢ When you finally get to meet your appointment, look them in the eye and shake their hand firmly. Don't try to wrestle him to the ground but don't leave him with the impression of a dead fish either.

➢ Thank him for the opportunity to meet with him. It doesn't matter if you had to chase him down for the last month, thank him.

Get off to a good start. Remember, the clock is ticking.

Good Intentions

I am always bemused by the phrase, "I had intended to do it but … ." You can fill in the blank with anything and everything. When you hear someone proclaim they had intended to do something, they are actually saying it was just not important enough to really matter to them.

Dreams come true only when you pursue them. Intentions become reality only when you act on them. All those good intentions won't carry any weight when measured against results that are not there. Turn your intensions into actions. Write them down, explore alternatives and anticipate roadblocks that may hinder you. Then move forward. Try. Don't just intend to try - whether it's your business, your community or your family. The world is full of good intentions. We need more results.

Good intentions just aren't good enough.

Who Took Notes?

You had a lengthy conference call covering the plans for your presentation. Yet, a week has passed and nothing has happened. You thought everyone understood their respective tasks, but somehow none of them are done. What went wrong?

Perhaps no one was taking notes. Or, if they were, no one shared those notes with others on the call. Don't make the mistake of assuming everyone understood exactly what you said (or what you *thought* you said). You may even be questioning what was covered yourself. Despite the intent of giving the entire team clarity, the vision is now fogged. Like the game of telephone, each participant will come away with a different perspective of what's going to be done, when it will happen or who will do it. How do you avoid these problems?

➢ Take charge. Don't be afraid to be a leader. End each call with a summary of what was discussed, who is assigned specific tasks and when those tasks are to be completed.

➢ Let everyone know when the next call or meeting is to take place.

➢ Follow up each call in writing. Don't make it a long rehash of everything. Just the salient points covered in your verbal summary – who, what, where & when.

Tearing Others Down

Your mother always told you, "If you can't say something nice about someone don't say anything at all." We should all heed mom's advice. Unfortunately not everyone does. I'm not talking about critical analysis of a person's performance or a discussion of the merits of the latest sales proposal. I'm talking about personal sniping. Taking shots at an individual's personality quirks, decision processes, management style or mannerisms simply do not belong in the workplace. There is nothing to gain and everything to lose by "badmouthing" others. Sooner or later, your sniping will catch up to you. Contrary to what you might think, you can never build yourself up by tearing others down. Sniping doesn't make you a bigger person, only smaller. The best result you can expect by slamming others is to come across as a sour, pitiful person. Trust in you will diminish and, as a result, you will be less effective.

Avoid the entire area of office gossip that demeans or belittles others. You don't have to become a Pollyanna or paste a permanent smile on your face. However, there are things you can do to avoid potential problems.

➢ Keep the conversations and remarks to business issues.

➢ Avoid stereotyping anyone based on appearances or hearsay.

➢ Remember, what goes around comes around.

Mother was right after all.

Running on Empty

One of the brightest men I ever worked for
was also one of the worst workaholics I'd
ever met. Perhaps the two went together,
perhaps not. He was an absolutely brilliant
individual who knew the business and
everything that made it tick. Yet he often
stumbled when it came to working with
others in the organization and that stumble
eventually cost him his job. The man was
so focused on work, he lost sight of
everything else. He had little tolerance for
anyone who didn't work as hard or as long
as he did. He considered vacations as
"necessary evils" in business. He missed
the point. He was running on empty and
didn't know it. He didn't work to live, he
lived to work – and the work consumed
him.

Drive and ambition are terrific attributes,
but only if tempered by balance and

diversity. Work hard, but play hard too. Take time to unwind and recharge. Not only will you physically feel better, your focus and drive will be stronger.

Remember, if you run on empty long enough, you won't be running at all.

Eye to Eye

I recall interviewing one young man for a position in a client's company. During the entire interview he seemed to be focusing either on the notepad in my hand or the cup of water in front of him. I doubt he looked me in the eye more than two or three times and when he did, it was only for a moment. He didn't get the job. On paper and over the phone he seemed well qualified. However, in person he lacked spark and intensity. Worst of all he couldn't articulate himself in the most basic fashion or look at the person with whom he was talking.

The eyes are the window to the soul. Unless you look at someone when you talk to them, you won't know if your message is getting through. You will miss the subtle responses to your comments. You won't be able to "see" recognition or affirmation to your words by staring at your shoes. Fixing the problem is right before your eyes.

Focus on the person with whom you are speaking. If you are talking to a group of people, look each one in the eye for a moment or two while you're speaking then move on to the next person. When you're listening to some one speak, pay attention to the individual by looking them in the eye. Not doing so is not only rude, it implies you aren't interested in what they are saying.

The eyes have it.

The Light of Day

You've been working all day on a special
proposal. You've racked your brain long
and hard to get everything spelled out in
exactly the right fashion. The hour is
getting late and all you want to do is finish
your masterpiece and put it in the mail.
You thought you had done a great job until
you are looking over your copy the next
morning. You then realize your finely
chosen words from last night really sound
like incoherent jabber. What happened?

Chances are you were so caught up in the
process, you didn't step back and objectively
review what you'd done. We all make this
mistake. Very rarely can we sit down and
get our thoughts out perfectly on the first
try. The press to clear mental roadblocks,
our fatigue, distractions or any one of a
hundred other reasons can cause us to miss

problems. So what can you do to insure clarity?

Put the work down. Go for a walk. Take a shower. Get a good night's sleep. Let all of the issues and emotion clear and then come back and review your effort. Errors you couldn't see yesterday will jump off the page once you look at them in the bright light of a new day.

Trust and Humpty Dumpty

Very few things in business (or life) are as
valuable or fragile as trust. When you have
trust in someone, you have confidence the
person or group will always act with
integrity. They will always do the right
thing. Likewise, when someone has trust
in you, they are confident you can be
counted on to perform without question.

Trust not only needs to be developed and
nurtured, but protected and maintained.
Trust is something that must be earned
everyday – something that may take years
to develop but only seconds to destroy.
Once shattered, just like Humpty Dumpty,
all the king's horses and all the king's men
won't be able to put it back together again.

Always be vigilant to not betray the trust
others place in you. Don't let your words or
actions compromise a relationship that took

so long to build. Disassociate yourself from those who violate the trust of others. If people hold others in such disregard, they are likely to do the same to you. An employee or coworker that cannot be trusted is someone to keep at a distance lest you, by association, become distrusted yourself.

Humpty Dumpty would probably agree.

Monday – Opportunity or Dread

The bumper sticker on the car in front of me read "I don't do Mondays". It said a lot about the driver – mostly negative. What do Mondays do to you? Do you dwell on the upcoming traffic snarled commute to work or the pile of paper on your desk waiting for you once you get there? Or do you see it as a new challenge, one more opportunity to shine?

Success is as much a measure of attitude as it is ability. If we see only the negative aspects of our jobs, we may get through the day, but we will be miserable doing so. Just as importantly, you will impact all those around you. Everyone you meet will pick up on your mood and act accordingly. If you are the manager, your staff will presume your demeanor is the attitude to have and will follow your lead. Is that what you want?

This doesn't mean you have to jump out of bed each morning and burst into song. You don't have to become an "over the top" optimist. However don't be a Simon Legree either.

Before you hit the office door or make the first phone call or even before you see your children off to school (they'll key off of your mood as well), reexamine your attitude. Focus on your day and week ahead as an opportunity, not drudgery.

Positive attitudes yield positive results.

Pulling the Trigger

We all face difficult, unpleasant tasks. One of those is to dismiss an employee. The anguish and agony of what I went through in the days leading up to one particular termination left me sleepless, irritable and literally sick to my stomach. When the time arrived and the event was over, I was surprised to learn the employee had been under similar stress. He knew things weren't right and also agonized over it. The outcome wasn't what he had wanted, but he was relieved it was finally over and he could move on.

Most of us face unpleasant situations with delay tactics. We hope by avoiding a problem, it will just go away. Some do, but most don't. What can we do?

> ➤ Put the problem(s) at the top of your 'to do' list. Don't let the situation

fester. You can't really focus on other topics while storm clouds are looming.

➢ Get your facts straight. Eliminate conjecture and opinion.

➢ Never act in anger. Never be impulsive.

➢ Make your decision and then take action immediately. Not next week, today.

Tough decision making is one area where leaders are separated from everyone else. Never fear pulling the trigger. Once the decision is made and acted upon, everyone can move ahead.

Smiling in the Face of Adversity

There is a twisted bit of wisdom which goes "The man who can smile in the face of adversity has thought of someone else to blame". We may smirk, but in many ways we know the phrase has become an all too common practice in today's world. When things go badly, we look for a scapegoat. We try to find someone (or something) to blame for the situation. We deflect even the slightest possibility this mess could be our own fault – that we could have been responsible for any part of it. This kind of behavior has become nearly epidemic.

Being a leader doesn't mean you are always right. It does mean, however, when you are wrong you take responsibility. Being a leader means you do the right thing all the time, not just when it suits you. It means you own up to problems and issues that are of your own doing and then provide the direction to fix them. No one is perfect. We all make mistakes. Just don't compound them by shifting the blame.

Effort vs. Result

We all like to see people give their best effort whether the intent is to finish the race, score the touchdown or "go the extra mile". We admire individuals who really try in the face of enormous odds even if their efforts fall short of winning. Great in sports and philanthropic endeavors. Not so great in the everyday world of business.

That is not to say results, despite how we got them, are all that matter. There are laws and codes of conduct to follow. We can't be so focused on completing the tasks at hand that we lose our moral and social compass. The ends don't always justify the means.

Yet while we should all applaud the attitude and spirit of hard work, we need to be careful not to confuse effort with results. The bottom line is, after all, the bottom line. Results aren't measured by an almost sale, the nearly completed payroll or the almost finished production run. Even working sixty hours a week at a job doesn't ensure you of success. Results are measured by what was accomplished and not by what was intended to be accomplished despite the time and effort put into the task.

Effort is important, but results are what count. It's why they keep score in a ball game. It's how we keep score in the business world too.

Your Signature

The next time you are about to sign your name to something take a moment to reflect on what you are really doing. Your judgment, credibility and integrity are literally on the line – that one where your name is going. When you affix your signature to a letter, a report, a petition or a simple receiving form, you are telling those who read the document that you understand it. Furthermore, you approve everything the document says. From spelling to syntax to context to belief in the document's message, your signature says to anyone who might rely on the content that it's okay. That's a powerful statement.

Stop and take the time to think about what you're signing and why you're signing it. Disavowing a document bearing your signature after the fact is far too little far too late. By refuting a document after you sign it your credibility will, at the very least, take a "hit" and credibility is one thing to be guarded fiercely. Your "about face" will say you are backtracking on something you previously agreed to or, worse, you agreed to something you didn't understand and didn't take time to consider. Even if someone else had prepared the content, it won't matter. You signed it.

So, re-read that document before you sign. Your integrity is on the line